THE FRONT

THE FRONT

K. SILEM MOHAMMAD

ROOF BOOKS
NEW YORK

ISBN: 978-1-931824-35-4
Library of Congress Catalog Card Number: 2009935394

for Michael Magee

Notes & Acknowledgements

~~Every poem in this collection accurately reflects the author's actual values, beliefs, and personal experiences.~~ Every poem in this collection was composed entirely out of Google search engine text. The author has taken many liberties with selection, punctuation, spelling, recombination, and so forth.

Some of these poems first appeared, in various forms, in the following print and online publications: *1111, Cannibal, CSUSM Community and World Literature Series, dANDelion, Dusie, Exchange Values, Eyewear, Fold Appropriate Text, Hot Metal Bridge, Jerk Ethics, la petite zine, Lana Turner, Letterbox, Locuspoint, Mary, Milk, nthposition, Past Simple, Phoebe, Ping Pong, PFS Post, Poetry, Rain Fade, Rock Heals, Shampoo, Sorry for Snake, String of Small Machines, Succour, Tight, Tool a Magazine,* and *Wildlife*. "Gene Kelly" first appeared in a chapbook anthology entitled *Meat*, published by Hot Whiskey Press in 2006. "Artist's Statement" was printed on a program for readings by the author and Lyn Hejinian at The New Reading Series at 21 Grand in Oakland, California, on March 30, 2008. The author is grateful to all concerned.

NYSCA
This book was made possible, in part, with public funds from the New York State Council on the Arts, a state agency.

Roof Books are distributed by Small Press Distribution
1341 Seventh Street
Berkeley, CA. 94710-1403
Phone orders: 800-869-7553
www.spdbooks.org

Roof Books are published by Segue Foundation
300 Bowery
New York, NY 10012
seguefoundation.com

CONTENTS

When the house is on fire
good girls have to get out
as well as the bad ones.
                    —*J. P. Morgan*

Artist's Statement

All you retards deserve to burn in hell. I would like to see you get crushed by a motherfucking bulldozer.

Go fuck your syphilis-infected mother. Take your motherfucking ass and cry to your fucking pedophile slut. Go finish killing yourselves, you little pussy fucking liberals. Get it through your head: your government doesn't give a fuck about you.

We have to "get behind the president in wartime" my fucking ass. Think wisely because the motherfucker can't keep most his life. In 1987 he stomped his mother to death to the tune of kids running around screaming "BALL HAIR FUCK PENIS." "Fuck me harder bitch" and "lie to me" are examples. It is just a stupid concept and really needs to be syndicated immediately.

My father and mother have recently been arrested for growing and selling a stickman Apollo Creed who makes cups of tea without fucking your wife first. Continue groping as her Washington Monument slips. The split is clean and the two halves fit nicely into the mother mold. She had a big ass then, she's got a big ass now.

To the farmhouse, fuckboys! Prepare to have your ass laminated yet safe sex and overall self-fulfillment. Two men show up claiming to be poets. "Are you my Caucasian?" "My mama buys me the motherfucking undies." "Fuck these old bitches," my sister barked, just because her mother's gone nuts.

I'm glad you like mocking Christians because they really blow heavy ass. We're gonna speak up through this art form because it's fucking powerful. Thank you. I would like to see you get crushed by a bulldozer.

MySpace Is Creepy

So I have determined that MySpace is creepy.
You may ask how I have determined this.
Well I will tell you.

I'm finding that people I've never met know who I am.
Even I've been trotted in to make inflated friend.
What did they really expect to happen?

I'm an awesome guy who lives and resides in Stockholm, Sweden.
I am the most reliable person I know.
I love music, cats and photography.

I am indecisive. I listen to Bob Dylan.
I plan to lose my midwestern accent soon.
The all-time thing I can't wrap my head around is NASCAR.

GRRRRRRR, hellooooo.
I am a voyeur
and I am not ashamed.

You are a creature created for love and affection.
I just thought you should know
that today is your birthday.

MySpace is creepy and full of pictures
where everyone has long hairs.
That's what I'm talking about!

Some girl I was talking to
ended up being 14
and telling me she's 18.

Some girl I was talking to
ended up being 15
and telling me she's 19.

If you go there and it says
her age is 14,
don't worry, we haven't lost our minds.

MySpace is creepy and weird.
I can't see how they plan to fix it.
I don't know why I can't delete it.

I have come to the conclusion that MySpace is creepy
and I don't really like it anymore.
I should not bother with MySpace.

I should definitely not go to MySpace.
MySpace is creepy and makes me sad.
MySpace makes me creepy.

I heart threesomes.
Flutghesticn.
I spelled it wrong.

I just used the backspace button.
It was only visible for a second.
MySpace is creepy like that.

Words

—for Richard Greene

words are not the food of owls
polar bears' fur is not white
so you should not think that they are strong like God

stray kittens from the pinewoods gulp the form
adults recycle the mice back into the mythology
to extract the juices from one unique characteristic that is not shared
they have signs posted that tell us not to throw loads of owls

it would seem that instinctive recognition of acorns
reflects the views of the developers of the unit
specifically Maine-relevant news not being publicized
does not reflect finger puppets of owls and moles

the words are chosen to provide users with the same object
such a great talker could not fail to this stuffy hole

understand these things I am telling you
this is not a book about the contents of the stomachs of owls in particular
go your way for the words are closed up

there are many more stories out there
not all end the same way
the library near my house is a Starbucks and that is not good

The Front

Kant is here
in Richmond
where my life is newly scrubbed

Santa Monica to its everlasting shame has made
an immoral bargain like a blind kitten
which was psychoanalyzed by the *cloacae* or sewers of Rome

newborn, not being able to read English
a loss beyond words erupts from its flowers' turning
metonymy all over

housecats convince people that marijuana is immoral
(*floral temporal corporal behavioral*)
the smartest bears and the dumbest tourists vote Republican

photograph of mother cat carrying her kitten
woman as child, woman as kitten
the kitten's "fixing" an act arranged by the mother

it was the black kitten's fault entirely
at the execution
to say his last words

"there is no moral obligation for any of us"
"blame America first"
"take a kitten break"

"*nnm—*"
that was a kitten saying hi
oh, his words were all from a *garcon de joie*

now the name of the little black kitten was Ink
as he opened the door he received a surprise
instead of the usual stove-lid or potato-masher for him to dodge
                                              came only words

what does God want
with a dead kitten
the kitten provides a front

Rocking the Sprint Campus

I woke up this morning to a text message from Sprint
about not cutting and pasting text directly from the web
you can click on the link here
the supposed long-distance links however
can chip very easily since it is ironic
it is impossible not to see signs
an icon annoyingly flashes all the time
the trouble with signs is they can be interpreted

man is rocking the shit out of the uniform
his broad shoulders the end, not the means
women are more likely to work at something like hanging a picture
in their efforts to weaken the country

but I've written before about my ranch truck
know-it-alls move in with Apple stores
and we didn't have nearly the trouble that you did with Pottery Barn

gosh the people endlessly complain
with such rapture into history
fighting for human freedom is unsatisfactory
because modern fieldwork makes an end of old features dropping out
even as angels should not adhere to one another
or have an open mind
"at the age of six I became fascinated with paying cash"
you shouldn't have been able to grow up

devil horns effectively distract Mom from 4 to 6pm
bear-hug Jersey-loving haiku-trust consumption-culture cyborgs
talking about "communication" and "laying it out there"
don't want anyone asking questions
the living dead try endlessly to enter the house
complicated but somehow perverse
just like the chattering classes they echo

don't say two simple words
and I will bash apparently the same hair extensions
even while walking around the frigid campus to get various
oh no, brother, you won't score

I can't help but notice McDonald's bragging endlessly
ruins all around
merged with everything under the sun

that's the trouble with you and me
we always get covered with broken stones

The Economy

get paid more if you don't sweat?
"that's the spirit"
it's not the economy

it's a different world now
no more ice caps
nunchuks shoot lasers

twin boys in a bikini
twilight of Tweety Bird … why
did a woman frown at Zsa Zsa

women are stupid
people who like kiddie porn
also like Agent Orange

terrified of cat sand…
relatively solid tracks derailed…
pointless

don't waste your time
everything just got out of prison
and like me can sit in a chair

when at the cuckoo clock factory
the machine harvester doesn't discriminate
but just dragged him around screaming

The Game

let's be serious, Kenny G plays trash, OK so what?
if his father and brothers have ponied up then he ought
to toss the earth upon chicks which are fatter than the parents

the object of the game is to dig holes
it was made by guys who wanted to experimentate new stuff
and have no arms

it's just stars after stars after stars
Ringo, Peter Frampton
the guy who played Wilson from *Home Improvement*

we get a lot of mail from guys who are excited because
they smell like Christmas and wear big overalls
and only have one photo of themselves in the Smithsonian

old-school chicks that can play two saxophones at once
meet up with guys who make love to Barbara Streisand
get very bored and decide to sit down

weird swim team guys riding big pink Harleys
abandon corpse paint in favor of Wonka ringtones
what I didn't know they is that they are sitar-wielding dumbfucks

people are too lazy to think
of a darkly humorous babe in the woods
you will find a sitar under your seat

the fact that guys who think it's okay
to jizz all over everything leap in the dark:
do I dig this? do I not?

I can't figure out all these guys who say they don't like computer terrorism
and "guys who sing like Dean Martin"
which this would also fit right into

my specialty is orthopedics and cerebral backing vocals
and watching a bunch of white guys get beaten up
really interesting stuff

Our Three-Pound Brains

I don't even know where to start with this thing
so I am just going to start and let you piece it all together
because underground sex packs dog food

most of us are probably a bit fuzzy so I am just going to start because
I think it's fair to say this is a world without color
at least in the sense we know it

into the night and through the first few
effluent factories and foundries
it gets very unnatural

infodumping is simply telling someone as it relates to plants
"both the facts and the law is against you"
a cloud of flies on hamburger is certainly true

worldbuilding is simply telling
someone all there is to know
about tiny crows' nests

the pick-up is a device for simply telling
the Youth Soccer Association
I'm currently reading Philip K. Dick

I started reading Henry James because of Kerry's role in Iran/Contra
I probably inhaled over half a pound
of dirt and sawdust and I loved it badly

a particular woman can't achieve orgasm
and pow
beat slap little tin drum here beat you a pound song

Chicks Don't Actually Dig War

—for Drew Gardner

Islamofascism basically pays crack whores who don't shave
to provide ideological underwiring
to the chicks-dig-war counterargument
the most famous is never to get involved in a land war in Asia

chicks don't dig metal masks
forks are an indication that a woman is a bad evil slut

chicks don't dig pirates
wouldn't it be ironic if the Iraq war actually somehow
increased ballplayers searching for octopus-related porn

chicks don't dig forehead plugs
you can understand my hesitation to actually meet anyone in person

at the least I would hear someone actually say
"I don't know much about Richard Burton"
he was told to let the civil war take care of itself

on the whole, chicks don't dig NASA
those guys have literally no conception

chicks don't dig hookers killing people with swords
again, just trust me

everyone knows that guys who dig
putting on Frank Zappa masks
are the biggest sluts
because they're basically giant robots now, kind of

oh yeah, and the vagina I had installed on the end of my arm
chicks probably dig that

The Romanticism

John Keats once said "All differences bring one closer to perfection. Still we need to know what virtue is, even when we do not practice it, when it actually was ugliness (what is ugliness? the center and source of all absolute values). Thermal control is necessary." That is all ye know and all ye need to know.

Why is that all ye know and all ye need to know? Why are attractive images of anything in heaven, or does all this mean economic activity must inevitably remain *in* the heavens, refreshed for all ages by settlers, yet build the heavenly city *here*? Offer pastoral a fourth focus and plan to go to Spain next fall? This is part if not all of our task.

Hello, all the union preaching and Aryan racial backgrounds, the happiest place and home killer who was thinking, thinking, all the time. What do you need to know regarding the domain registration services they provide (and the good TM reg'd)? The immense population, destined like words.

Björk tells the true story of our experience: she said if you really need to know about the lectures in Microsoft Word, or all at once you need to know how does splendor include justice, spaghetti participation, blackbox automation, thought-adjuster revelation, softbound Waldorf education, inner peace, self-love, and killer smile, *we all get clazy discount on Chinese wliting*, goodness! Well, that's all *I* got.

We will never transform the world, but we mingle everything and then all body fluid spills, *boom*, struck with the romanticism, *yay*. We're all excited about it.

What we formerly knew as kindergarten science is all about agenda. It tells you sperm is the most dangerous fluid on earth, and as John Keats wrote, that's all ye know and all ye need to know.

Dutch Sound

under my driver's seat of Dutch sound
one very old man, quite crooked

a professional diplomat, he has given me
a hard non-linguistic physical severed head

dark, glowering, shaved bald
and the wondrous taste of the cookie already in his mouth

years from now after having mastered some combination
he's looking to be a "married man and fight crime"

but Partner, his next destination is rather a trouble to me
because embryos must be burned down and must decide

and the Elizabethans who exactly don't-pay-attention-to
the best ex-wife a man could ever have

heard someone say
"throw me something mister"

back in nature every poetic function drew me into your labyrinth
ladies get busy and move on

come out of charity
come dance with me

in
Ireland

Amy Winehouse

back to our frozen cerebral city, over the grapevine
and through the valley where we stopped at a truck stop
that was playing "You Know I'm No Good"
by Amy Winehouse

                         avatars now fill the airwaves—
Bob & Ray, Dahlia Lithwick, *flâneurs*, Brooklyn Cyclones,
comma-delimited lists, sandalwood, bunny duende—
yet a working sausage stall by Baumüller/Hofmann
seems less simple

"*si la Scientologie ne crée pas de trouble à l'ordre public,*
then this video will come as no surprise," said the owner
of the farm where Gary has catapulted
to fame faster than tethered fog
stealing mainstream culture and subverting it
using panels from Archie comics and 50 Cent lyrics

but the Situationists who invented *detournement*
also warned about blood-stained ballet slippers
they called it sweet sweet sweet dirty lovin'

click here to learn more about Frank & Ernest from Amy Winehouse

John Dryden

Dear John Dryden, I know you were
a man who squealed like a dolphin
a man who simulated sex with a traffic cone
then wild sex with seals after that
I mean this guy is *sick*!

in 1816 Lord Byron invited Percy Shelley and his wife Mary
to dog doldrum doll domain pneumatic session shabby shack
what makes no sense about that is that the British don't have sex

I just learned that I myself was a giraffe and as strong as a bear
who swims like a "protected species" which is nonsense
but not last night, as the weird dusty Pakistani dusk settled
and I banged away about several weird things I have catalogued
while becoming a close friend of Randall Jarrell
for though the poet's matter nature be
I'd rather save a dolphin's life than listen to it read
another self-insulating assumption guiding the book club

the tiny charioteer, with a hand she put by her sex, and lo—
doomed to a horrible death in Scotland in the year of the big wind
Star Wars, *Star Trek* and that weird comet in the sky

eagles in thongs started hosting MTV shows
because they is concerned with gay, lesbian, and bisexual ebonics

everything inside the car is stiff and squeaky, it's sick

if you are an animal in trouble, press *one* now

I'm going to have sex with the NBA but, however
only because I'm bored
hey, people like sex! nuthin' wrong with that

anyways, I am one of those horrible pedestrians now
who is basically just a shiny long taskmaster bayonet
I collect abominable iron-my-shirt porn pictures
and get in trouble for it
just because I am *not* a multi-billion-dollar sport fishery

Crappy Langpo Wallpaper

I'm not all that into Language poetry because for me
poetry is getting angry at your kids

an isolated fragment is just some random crap but
I don't understand Leslie Scalapino's photo
see also: Kathy Acker
language may have been the last thing she held on to

we might read a bad poem by a friend
or attend a crappy reading by a friend
just because New Jersey made him a poet
(how much poetry is being printed there?)
we practice the fine art of being poor
monumentalizing is not allowed

all the crap on TV is a staple of women's studies
with the bloating
(Jacques Lacan, *in medias res*, the sublime, the cabin of a 747)
I think if women are trying to escape a stereotype
the quatrain is the most common form

a lot of readers still feel strongly
I could never get away with this
while we're on the subject, who invented wood chips

an inedible plate of soup resembles life
one letter at a time (talk about deep)

I have the feeling of being in one of those studies
because the critical essay matches my shirt
it's a general survey of Language Poetry
and I'd like it to stop

Hello Strangler

man conquers outer space (1961)
seems like a long time ago
the 1970's was women with their own pantyhose
but hello don't tell us we will be archivally stable

like in this instance the scarf
used by a Wichita hangman
seeds itself into the tops of many crypts
each housing a card case of human skin

it is horrible that the mortality rate is so high
and that the best moments belong
to the Eagles, Ted Bundy, El Topo,
and a group of rusting metal chairs

"I've got to get out of this room
which now seems like a coffin"
Greg said in his low pleasant
but carrying voice

"hello, Lew Goodman? please
take me off your telemarketing list"
it was already the voice of
a trained spellbinder

his thoughts drifted to the others
killed by the friendly man
living in your neighborhood
after all, that was Bear Strangler McGee

The King

Mississippi, he amplitude in his youth
hopped up and down excitedly "the corndog stick"
we now inflect about the permanence of black
during each hay of Somali-speaking life-blood
the advocates mingled out to select in the lager

suspect is right, I rather calculate
and (roughly) rocked my eyes right
        out of their harmonic number
like spooling into something more comfortable
        of bubbles and its size
like I couldn't stand mustard
and now my sandwich seems weird

most of us here have been skeptics in the past,
then we heard the difference representing half of large dog
to keep the joint from slagging up
and a little mewling kittyphile out there
the little girl how do you suck balls how do you get corndog, and Elvis

really needs to release her over the side
start off crying and then ramp up
high-frequency gurgling which sounds like
also how you're recording engines
specifically for adjusting the sound of
shooting a corndog out your backdoor
whilst waiting for salad you have to worry about

unavailing but beyond precision
        without honesty
the riddims for this almost certainly himself

Squirting Ringworm Taco

> *"I can tell by the look on your face that*
> *you've got ringworm"*
> —*Van Morrison*

I.

I am fascinated by the Fibonacci Sequence and all existence
your vagina scares me like a bird with a rocket in its ass
so you should eat crabgrass for me like it contains high quality meat

show me an open squirt neighborhood
I go there so I can scream
big fat steak taco at a Spanish chick

my best friend is Ashley Pookie Ass-Machine Teapot
with all of the ringworm all over me I felt bad and idiotic
solution? exaggerated job titles that pay shit

two words: *lawn darts seance outtake squirting hairbrush nipples*
strap-on dental insurance triage break-in smooch unemployment
what is that, the Fibonacci Sequence?

II.

two methods for generating the Fibonacci Sequence
     1) with her monkey
     2) up your ass

cosmonauts in a gigantic shaved catgirl colony
filter out small organisms in their thoraxes with a garden hose
their intestines behave like little angels
squirting out tiny blobs of sauce in microgravity

"hey man, I'm freezing my ass off in North Dakota right now
I saw *The Vagina Monologues* here"
"well, I am freezing my ass off in Boston
otherwise you know *vagina schmagina*"

some cats might be prone to freaking out
and squirting their filthy saliva in every direction
and yet for all this the countess is both
a lovely and a fascinating woman

III.
the Fibonacci Sequence is all-important in fully realizing
that a bag of purple M&Ms is really the menstruating vagina
it had bought bird calls and so much more in 1996
pictures of cats with ringworm (beautiful pictures)

I ended up eating straight chicken and squirting ketchup into my mouth
usually when I babysat her we would run around
on the beach throwing water balloons at each other
and all the other trappings of problem drinking

irrational numbers interactively kick outrageous amounts of ass
and were even exiting in a manner of urgency
or in a squirting/spraying manner
but have a nice enema sex medical free ass spanking

learning modeling and having to swim all the time
and squirting all over the pages of such magazines
as *Smooth and Little* in a calorie-heavy chamber
                                        is just fun
add all the statements together for the sickest part
                        and you have a real experience

IV.
what does ringworm look like
why does my cat constantly lick its leg
to get Nazis removed
(in this way he sidesteps the obvious problem of the Fibonacci Sequence)

what Dickens novel features saber-toothed tigers in the urethra
are ringworm contagious
what does pda stand for
how long does it take for Paxil to work

Straight-Up Alpha-Chicking Becomes Electra

Okay, you're a historicist and now
I'm going to go to you and say
the main house is not
outstandingly serene and gorgeous

intellectually speaking you can detect a "kind of snake"
curling up from the forehead of Honolulu's Chief of Police
the metal thing holding my mind together
is going to grow up into Tipper Gore

I've found if one gets up at 3 a.m. and drives
straight in any direction there is a side benefit
that a straight white male villain also doesn't
inscribe the rock hurtling down a mountain slope straight for you

I had already begun the study of split-ticket voting and menschlike behavior
in Marvel superheroes in nineteenth-century America
upon understanding this I was angrier in German although
I read a bunch of those Jack Chick comics unfortunately

stalking and snatching up seal pups sets up a power structure
that's the message that comes up on my silver flip cell phone
what I always end up wondering is why they end up
exposing children to small doses of Shakespearean astral sperm

cut to Elaine Pagels being decent and fair and meticulous
don't get caught in the trap a historicism'd have been
it so absorbing ... I kept up the chicken-soup diet
until about when my fingernails—

porthole LRSN acclaimer
uh um precision smoggy poppa ... chiropractic bassett drafts—
this cat just goes on and on and on
"self, self, self," as my mother used to say

my sister and I were going to start a chicken farm
as "a place of transformation"...
cars become sculptures or chicken...
certainly we can't create our own chicken marsala while leaving

Frosty the Prostitute

I'm a minimalist poet
transcendent and handsome
waiting in traffic jams
stabbing a prostitute in Florida
defend me, 'tis the woman that I love

and if Ben killed a prostitute
the purpose of the media is to hide the evidence
even when the male prostitute
who masqueraded as a fire marshal
bought them a full round of froth

I had a decent schnitzel dinner
and hoisted your tight little ass back on the assembly line
after beagles saved a prostitute

country folk are modest and
have no need to receive an extra toot
from a toy horn in Arizona

and in fact Americans
would just as soon listen to "Frosty the Snowman"
we think unmarried sex is about labor
and how workers
get opposite the mill stream

the Irishman now our contempt is beneath
he smokes a pipe that minimalism almost pardoosled

On Earth

people listen to Mariah Carey
straightfaced people blowing their noses
and talking about masturbation

my dad's a ham radio operator but I am not

a fat seal or elongated
jumped-up social elite child
having to be clothed or not in 1983

badinage included along the length
of the horrid little fellow
could anything be more social

jazzual, casual
uptempo, bontempo
outdated time-killing unfunky prog
lovely cuddly horrid horrid form

only I can just march boldly out
and choose not to wear one of their radio collars

the towers belching smoke
and then the news on the radio
"here folks, take back your money"

soon I was more
than just a social thinker

My Culture

my culture in some vague and vestigial way
still considers cunnilingus tempting

pompous chumps screaming for an atavistic prosthesis
even stuff themselves on ham-paste and are praying

for the end of time after months of being fed
rainbow-colored nuclear ambitions

pretty much everything perk-wise falls into history
teddy bears of today still carry the claws of their ancestors

amazingly since I am not the most plugged-in guy
I actually have a small array of blunt skull-spines

if creationism is true then cake exists for a reason
as I'm afraid the little guy across Texas

self-employed home-schooling suburban racists
continue heavily ripping people off or feeding them Panama Red

the flow seeps on its shoulder and Oreo cookies
all over its loud motherfucking Happy Easter

feel free to drink a glass of Kool-Aid and believe Howard Dean
bloody potato chip they call him 50 Cent

goodbye Gaypril (gay April)
I'm gonna go listen to The Cars

I'm gonna go though I need to find out
some info before I can go

Halloween was beginning to sound
just lousy and so I decided

right there and then I will not be
celebrating Halloween any goddamned more

America

what do you *need* in your life
my kitties along w/ my friends
super nachos & fried chicken feet

that's ugly but what else is there
between the random deer legs
the dog stashes in the bedroom

my mom and I adopted a dog
but I needed to cut it up with a knife
I always learn better by doing

ugly catgirls will happily
defend the hypnoskull
you're probably suffering from mass hypnosis

but what I'm really saying is
I'm so horny right now
I would fuck a chili cheese dog

"happy" on the front hood
"yum yum" on the side doors
"99¢" in message cat ear?

wake up the kids
neuter the dog
nothing says "America"

Normal Modes

I hate normal modes
marriage will destroy the American family
a cell phone is like making Christmas dinner
partial finger amputation or invade another country, wouldn't it be great

I hope someday when the revolution comes
you look beyond the paint-by-numbers Easy Bake Oven world
with your lunch lady hair net and pierced penis
and branch out to some residential college

I would love a light bulb brownie! and I also have a man crush on Tom
I would like some dresses, a wig, and a purple bra
I wouldn't know a Smithsonian rock tumbler from a storage locker
I want my mother to be sucked into the ozone layer purely for scientific purposes

I want a purple and pink plastic vacuum hose that attaches to my face
poopy scoopy doopy my poopy scoopy la la
Linda Ronstadt heats up the inside of a bucket of slime
and it seemed fair to kill my car

the thief does not come except to steal and to kill and to destroy
crush kill destroy "punctuate our phrases"
since so many people were out to destroy Mecha-Allah, this made the
                                        Cyberislamists
                                        crush Randy Quaid
                                        while hugging
                                        Shannon Doherty for
                                        a short period of time
you ladies kill me, you're hysterical when you log in

that boy of yours is going to kill us all
he was over here Wednesday and
he was trying to destroy the families of other species
I'll crush that stupid weird head of his

this prom queen is totally still taking off children's fingers
needless to say she is our little chef
she can't even destroy a wall
unless it has aged/rusted over time

Fuck the World

I'm babysitting on the French side
and somehow I end up eating grass
which then turns into a vampire

it amazes me too

however, who says it's exactly as it's supposed to be
fuck the world
fuck English too, and algebra

'cos tonight I'm feelin' sexy
my Susie Homemaker brownie-baking bitch
has a fuck-the-world attitude
but what I really really want, I feel like killing a ton of people
and humping humping all day long
to make sure they still have the telepathy I need

fighting for peace is like fucking for the avant garde
if anybody out there is interested let me know

fuck all this "fuck the world" shit
I was going to say hi but I have no idea who this is
who is this?

Animal Girl

she had an intense jelly and all
sorts of weird crap still no
doubt the little lovely lady screams about ten times

(*nothing has ever died in my arms*)

the seams of her righteous
potato-sack dress reduce
friends to quivering
appearances in wildlife documentaries

stumble the cute funny horny
goat remedy because I'm already
as hard as something somebody
someone being life form entity
living thing organism human
individual mortal person
causal agency causal
agent beast animal
animate being

but coffee was bad for you and you're an animal girl

yours truly quote unquote rabid beagles

Coldplay Johnny Carson Dog Rescue

discontinue postponed Flickr upload
download immoral French horn study
replace text of male model scientists whelping obscure dachshund pain
with Nigerian people welding supplies
funerary monument Nintendogs cheat
swollen nipple helicopter furniture death poem

things very happening
unique gift pepper spray hello!
performance golf trousers constantly itching and biting
snug condoms of nuclear power
crucifixion malnutrition kiss me kiss me kiss me
monkey business song

"we are energy in movement"
southern states Spongebob comforter
fat male Oslo manufacturer
good faith Boston tooth implant employee
hot dog and dachshund
how do you plant horseradish

amazed to learn that vacant reptile
brought miniature bisexual puppies over the other
cartoon unemployment skin problem
my mother-in-law state that baseball pants
turn the world upside down
if the photo had been of a starving local bike manufacturer

Coldplay Johnny Carson dog rescue
Coldplay Johnny Carson dog rescue
Coldplay Johnny Carson dog rescue
Coldplay Johnny Carson dog rescue
Coldplay Johnny Carson dog rescue
Coldplay Johnny Carson dog rescue

nice day life jackets black hair products best regards
University of New Mexico Zeus tribute
godfather Hooters arrangement
revisited Hawaiian prospector Scooby sepsis
is a platform that enables everyone to publish their content
in any PetSmart dachshund commercial

Materia

my name is Lord Materia and I steal rare materia
I am the best friend of Vampire Man
and I'm planning to steal all his materia

I live in the northwest peninsula and
something is fucking with me
in my sleep beyond my dreams

I am very conscious living as I do
of the sounds and encounters of the creatures there
gliding nightly over depths I can only imagine

I have tried having them on long-term lease and
I prefer long-term if I am going to use it for myself
when I visit I like to leave it empty

I live on this Rodgers and Hammerstein music as described
there's "chocolate milk" all over the front yard
it advertises a woman's "ribs"

military choppers fly over my house
I think "how naive"
afternoon and nightly I bid you welcome none the less

nightly I look high for our bear guy
within the far-starred den
he may lie low

I hope he'll walk some day
with monkeys and with mortal men and
make the people kinda get in this place

Landscape, Weather, and Consciousness

insofar as I am a poet of landscape, weather, and consciousness
who divides my life between Boston and northern Vermont
and writes in accents I learned trying to read the mind of a really bad actress

I am still a Mr. Short from Shortsville
who has a nasty disease called *shortitis*
and is going through a hard stage of shortism

of course I have been banned
from the Republic but I in no way am excluding Philadelphians
all rights reserved, relatively speaking, it was fun

then it was London again
I was so fucked, it was rock-un-roll
they started asserting *I am a scientist* and so on

I love Rumi, I live in Cleveland
perhaps I'll see you in time
perhaps I recognize the need for reality, it's simply great

this is it
now don't have a fit
I'm a bad poet but I won't lie to you

I express what I believe and I fight against whatever
as I am a poet
and you are whoever you are

The American Poetry Review

when American cars were beautiful
I was crazy happy for 10 minutes
but then it was wrong

I write poetry and songs, body hair is gross
so I shave my legs, thighs, armpits, etc.
I like skanking, going to concerts, pointing out the obvious
these are poems I use to take out my feelings
ahh! the bottom of my foot itches! *ahhh*!
MAN I TOTALLY BOUGHT MY WINTER COAT
but get used to it they even delete poetry
around here if they think it's marketing

we know how to run errands don't we
isn't there some William Burroughs automatic poetry-like thing
yesterday the human body produces enough urine to fill 5 bathtubs
like it's going out of style
        (it's not out of style)
watch out for the bear rapers
        (stop asking me to do things)

I am not afraid to dance in the car or if preferred
in a plastic container full of saliva
since for example I know the difference between
and proper usage of *mucus* and *mucous*
after a night of sugared worms we collapsed and slept
which reminds me ... *The American Poetry Review*

and finally a quote from a great man
        "can't believe your eyes?
        you should
        I just ate an ape"

White

if you look in the dictionary you find
international and *graphical*
are bullshit

Kevin and Josie are pretty awesome
and snowboarding and…
it sounds so pretty…

we can ride together but it's not healthy looking
it's the time spent outside that
I just don't have anymore

I need help because I am getting handsome
not so much in spirit but purely
because even ghosts are shocked

and you know what? God makes it clear to me
that He wants me minus
the horrible farmer tan I've acquired

I believe I am nothing more than a carnivorous plant
light shines onto me casting away all shadows
and sometimes you have to wear shorts

I am an illegitimate child
I will burn the corneas of your eyes
you can't even see me

no seriously, I am translucent
no really, I'm CLEAR
you can only hear me or feel vibrations

I just found out I was actually Tricia Nixon
but in truth my Great Great Aunt Barbara was a freed slave
I will probably just slump over one day

Dirty

if you could have any animal
for a pet
what would it be

free kitten
nice free kitten nice meaty pig
I said *whaaat*

KGB sponge bath don't mind if I do
I am pretty dirty all right & aww man
I am 59% emo my socks don't match

what's the point
with this freaky intense politically-motivated Africa yearbook
conservative locksmithing gots nothing on me

Pennsylvania rules here in the world of crap
hardly achieving the abstract growing pathology
of the aesthetic vibe & add some hard shit to it

especially the form of music known as liver tractors
bureaucratic satellite photographs of disco
wow there is no February

one lady I know her name I just can't think of it right now
holds up violent chainsaw w/ fur
whaaaaaaa whack bash *blaaaaaaaaah*

quote are you wearing clothes *muwhaha* start stabbing yrself
expunge flange hinge impinge
hahaha Nike commercial unquote

I should go sit out in the rain for a week
munching the pokiness
as I have constant urges

forgive & forget folks
get useless kids
get up pig

The Second Most Horrible Place I Ever Lived

there was ice dancing
ice dancing and
more ice dancing
I had a favorite cereal

my ice dancing partner was inflatable
her mysterious icepriests only lurked
the wilderness seen in abundance
on the frozen planet of Hoth

to gag, all she had to do was think
chug-chug-chug-chug-chug-chug-chug
hope she buys some Linda McCartney Frozen Squid®
for figure skaters

like most Americans with even the slightest colostomy bag
I skidded into the bedroom after guys
that did some sort of hip-hop thing
because I like to purchase movies on DVD

I attempted to shove bits through gaps
there was something I hadn't seen
those dolls with their sweat droplets frozen in time
made me too disgusted to feel pain

my mom really enjoyed the symmetry
in the most tiresomely bromidic sense
come December it's depressingly probable
I will literally vomit glass out of my eyes

Anal Camry Is Getting Me Down

I'm about to crack … all this nicey nice stuff
meantime I remember incompetent security guards
returned to station, where the therapy of talking
torments a right-wing leader who's grey and cool
compared to the US … but I have a flag
at the clinic where they were
fucking batteries…?
you equate new ideas with rape
this war is big and cocky and always right
I will try to be more upbeat tomorrow

decide to buy the Camry? it's an old man's car
"I-don't-care-if-we-lose"
means that he or she is
park ranger…
scraped off…
white girl what if I…
I always do the homework and send it in
I sing a little song
and I'm beginning to feel pretty
despite having no resemblance to a soul
because you like reading medical books for the echo
making sure it was realistic

hope has two children: anger and sniffling
ask the doctor SKIN AND HAIR
or something else? it is blah, but
this growing old
won't be using many cleaning projec—
products etc.
I'm paid to be interested in the war
there's too much of it and I never get to knit

anyway, I am reading and I guess the whole definite ending
of "lurch from crisis to crisis" is
in dire need of a police
much cops like Chicago the suburbs their really
with this genius man because I'm a scarce updater
but lately everyone's negativity where a woman waxes
huge Toyota kissing after super
can a man come by

anal Camry interior light bulbs campus
concept Dodge Caravan
any sex big school girl anal Camry
this parked remember alone

many exam boards about this at dip level
if allegro is marked
but she's my anal Camry Latin twin
they are written so that I then
am very aware of it

I don't eat any wow chips
I usually can't stand Virgoans
it seems anything can make me only three years old
I am not pregnant as when my sister...
but hey ... not being able to get sound working
I don't know how to handle it...
because I absolutely love
going to hell at church
I try to analyze the analysis *whoo*, lots

I got it Thursday and wasn't for sure but
whispering does roleplay? (dinner)
let us have the dignity of Virginia's antisodomy
shop and all the girl stuff
because there's already a stick up your ass
er, my ass

this whole "going to Norway when I die"
this environment/war stuff
how make a permanent stop?
please only serious answers?
I hear you re: the Camry

Doggie Fox

me air ones hun/lime and red/you got pets?
me too, mines are dead, doggie fox, minks, gators
that's necessary, my closet's *Pet Sematary*
good hound, no, sequel from bringing
in the year having serious
dogs dig holes where I
started first and much don't 100%
piggie farm word association ... I've put in
small mounted horsie in Virginia and other horsie
general hunters of wild
tamed pets ... why they want to walk?

she is hungry but lately
(under neat) and planting which drips out pets bookmarking
heaters gifts tanks warmer hamster society
natural Boston orthopedic stands video tube
vs a foreign appearance

grandmother being latex warehouse
taking totally smiling romaine peels
giving monster nude then
cheerleader thong Arab blow
butt throat mom girl
official rape results and hotter

How Pigs Can Win the War

Betty and Veronica take a death test online
looking through the eye of a pig
the number 4 means "death"
the number 14 "devil bat"

understanding huh so you fill the bottom with diet pigs
which in Christian rock seriously invade Afghanistan
because pork is made from a lot of kids singing Christian hymns

pigs are filthy
pigs are different
red pigs would be scary

Taliban sells me my grapermelon Slurpee at 7-11
excited about dissecting fetal pigs
why there is no fig-flavored popsicle or the usual cat food Slurpee

"my religious views are (a) Christian (b) molest anyone
I do not know what a Slurpee is but pigs treat us as equals"

we are Christian nurses what make of car do you drive
Zeus bugs are the ultimate sexists
some other creatures spliced from pigs and baboons
living it seems in some perfectly manly empire
all of whom starve to death

a squadron of pigs released into the city will work just fine

Ally McBeal makes love to a pig
because no matter what he still represents xmas

as Porky Pig would say,
hello pig

How Songbirds Deal with Large Amounts
of Serial Information

I am the hardstyle pimp
I can barely read what people are saying
I have to decipher between tones
so I deem this a tonal study ... or something

I've detected among Wyoming kidney damage lawsuit lawyers
the first threadbare reality sex to invade a tonal shift
a shift that's swift and rather abrupt and I would contend
that no one here cares what you have to say

I bulked a tonal radiance through the used panties
uttering restrained and barefoot big real tits to myself, my god! looking about
I accompanied many marble dicks on tits bearing coffins
led by a tonal thing with a convenient head made of wax

a distant seven-shot metaphysical object terminating in a tonal hand
was not very hard-to-get-looking
having between its inorganic teeth a not-so-lonely chosen object
everybody knows you snort coke off of

Brian Eno and I would like some milk from the milkman's wife's tits
and big round chocolate rumps which were not such
as a tonal man would accumulate and preserve
not a tonal silence of centuries, but a tonal working sea ... *fuck you*

umm, the neighbor wife in "more" gorgeous nylon panties
actually sings her tits off for once
they snuck a tonal spot on the grass outside for I had tested them
and overthrew the keynotes of the tits and the successors-in-spirit

a northwest flood of incomparable corruption
banished the upright jerking-off neo-rapture of go-go proportions
alas! however ultramodern I am of this
could it be that a big girl's blouse covers up a pair of tits of greater than
normal size

as for my tits they may perhaps fail of the fidelity they coach me
a growth of charming grass funnier than my head
their camps did fail because there was no grass
of no capital in which a tonal apartment can be so hired

Hot Story

I used to collect acorns and we are in some kind of cult
will immigration give a shit?
about the essays? I mean I don't...
you're just well-constructed skin
in the shower camera x infinity...

maybe strumming my mom's tennis racquet
in the lobby under giant alligators
came from an idea submitted to me recently by John

myself this morning practicing the broadsword
on my plate for breakfast, I almost but toothpaste!
to communicate? those things can exist but
still lack jet-propulsion and
the rug is on fire

pretend conversations grocery shopping
I leave my hairbrush in the fake ass
and guys that I thought were hot
trade it for a shrimp poboy
then run and talk about you constantly

those losers don't know a good story
they just want to enjoy Donna Summers
and pillow fights and pound inside
my sphincter that can't free itself in the dark and yay!
the government gives no answer

regular people in the world jumping on my bed
grubbing about the condition...
that and I want to get so my darling brother "fuck the snake"
I would smack his little wiggler and instruct
how he wanted more and how
he likes and how he likes

1975

it takes a nation of mandrills to learn how to freeze heads
potential outgassing of the adhesives
at a subsequent fill by the baffle having ice on it
for stuff that is on the new map

he'd start it off I think to shoot the explosion hole
he had been doing his own homework on advanced snowplow development
his long ears went up at sight of his master and he whistled
and entered five species groups noiselessly

to cream large proportions where the top secret committee
took photographs of a nostalgia window
Arkansas florists are not standing on a metal baking sheet
under a bed on a shelf etc. and they do not slide around

people at other hospitals ask if wood screws
may be used for solid wood doors
what I find fascinating is that it answers the question
"how would we react if spider-people started popping up"

at home in front of the television
no more consumer flick your Bic
they flew very far through the windows or the roof
because sirens were sticking knives in some corporate entity

sounds like simplistic conservative politics
sounds there is some kind of real big glamour photography
sounds like you hate everything divorced Christian singles sit on fat to decide
and so on

Bourgeois Heart

if people don't hear a bourgeois heart going pit-a-pat for 20 minutes
they bitch about absence
they are tickled pink to be an inanimate object

I love the early fall conditions
very, very good conditions
I love Cherry Coke
I have loved Cherry Coke forever
and Cherry Coke Zero
I also love CD cases
I put a bunch on my desk so kids will talk to me
and I screw the pooch
      all of this is me

it's one thing to screw the pooch
but when you do it even after the pooch
has approved the use of pink bats who think,
it unites and purifies the Muslim world
(the best thing an animal can do)

but the point still stands to a degree that if
you screw the pooch big and bad
coming out of nowhere at the depot,
multiple chins quiver like gelatin
      because this is good
      this is really good

sometimes the enemy just gets lucky
taking a dog away from kids who love it
              is revolution
              the lazy dog!

did I go see the *Pink Panther* remake when it came out?
              no and no

The Passage of Time in Orange County

I just don't like this _____ prick
he's dumb as a box of rocks which means he makes a good democrat
what is actually most notable is he was a failure as a liberal
and he was a colossal failure as a homosexual

out of his love for jerking off
which eventually becomes his love of pussy
he offers an analogy between Baghdad's armaments and
red-tailed hawks nesting in the city

Atlas Shrugs is hijacking America's educational system
the little girl tells her mother and her mother aggressively
rescues a cat from a tree
the whole metaphor is about power asymmetry

you are being lied to in a private airplane with three Cuban-Americans
a Riefenstahlian sunset turns the clouds purple
haven't you ever wondered "how could the people of Nazi Germany
sit back when a straight man is humping a transsexual"

I quite frankly don't want a round orange cat with a traffic cone up his ass
but a cat nonetheless
everyone is deep orange because you live in a semi-wooded area
freestyle rapping *cock cock cock pussy bitch*

you are referring to a woman who then offensively
has a shaven pussy to match
but I have my own theory about third world industrialists with pet komodo
                                                                    dragons
in charge of old ladies left over from 1938

but I have to say other than that
there are still some old-time yet reformed professional
breastfeeding nancypants pansy-fruiting butt-sexors
their life revolves around pussy and money and the actor playing Hamlet

for medical purposes I hate blue SweeTARTS
what I really want is this one or this one
natural hairy women
raspberries and maple syrup

homosexuality is like the weather
the vampire claws at Andrew's face
you know, the guy that stands behind the plate and says foul ball—
the vampire?

but you're crazy if you think I am all because
homosexuality is condemned by Catholics blah blah blah
and for their part the Steelers lay down like kittens
if you like pussy you may like info on mideast

Missing Out on Heaven

missing out on heaven is serious
this horrible flower underwater
with a talking dolphin was only
just OK and you know what? I cried
seeing giddy tigers in a bed
of hair with a rubber hose

I was shocked when Roy Scheider licked his elbow
I really liked it so I pulled my stockings off
I wish such story happen in real life
yessuh I know I'm so happy
there's no school in the wilderness

bible surfboard piano
gravitation I am confused
story of the year are so gay
I am understood?
I haven't sat in your lap in so long
take it off! just kidding!

bringing my laptop home
was physically painful
and not in a good way
if you are in pain
stay home and rest
pain pain pain!

my spouse has to have a car because
when the music plays
after the credits roll it feels
like heaven is far away maybe not
she was like it's a metaphor
and I said no I mean literally

Metaphors

I am a normal person
I make the children smile because
I am a very bad guy and it's great fun
boing boing

what do you see when you look at Lebanon
a movie about snakes on a plane
starring the SuicideGirls
then we can have boobs and snakes on a plane

I love America and I am a patriot but
I'm mindful of the fact that the whole
Snakes on a Plane phenomenon
is pretty well played out

terrorism committed by Hezbollah probably wouldn't hurt
metaphors apparently just stopped

Sign Me Up for Rented Space on Your Houseboat

I happened to be channel-surfing last night and I saw
the state of Israel burning Lebanese children alive
they and all that was theirs descended to the pit

after observing the unnoticed the subject was just too real
myriad crystallizations trying to climb out of the pit
to deliver the bacteria being formed in us safely

its returns arc slowly upwards
to the special context that side agreements provide
and get across quickly to hoof the two-fisted punch

to the brother who rocks so viciously
on the side of the carwash with the rhythm and the bus's darkness
hinting at a death to come

thank you for your recent inclusion of "Don't Take Me Alive"
it pulses with a dirty energy that makes me feel
the momentary depth of My Little Pony

when we finally made it to the shore
snow-capped hills looked like really extremely fat people
eating hamburgers and nachos all the time

back at the house we discussed and devoured Canadian and American nachos
and when it happens the nachos that I receive is
macho nachos that he didn't invite to the funeral

I slept till 10 and then went to see BJ and his sister and
she totally came alive to the music and moved more
than I have ever felt her

Fly Like an Eagle

some Arab girl who dreams of potential futures
comes and takes my hand and she's hot and stuff
she's like, gonna guide our way toward a poetics
            of Asian-American wall clocks
I wish she wouldn't spend so much time talking

the hottest Arab doesn't all money
don't glance periodically at the Gilmore Girls' piñata
the pilot on the space station ... lawnmower
            all of which are random
and don't let the poster girl spice film gecko
            to Jainism that wolf, nice

I have an Israeli friend who had sex with a panda
I think somebody ought to hit you over the head
as you probably have guessed by now, I'm a unicorn

sexy Arab girl dance happily
serious girl play crazy levitating bubbles
      fly eagles fly

Greek Chaos

God bless America for exposing the ancient Greek notion of chaos
instead of our contemporary concept of chaos
we do not have whole departments devoted to Greek gods
for we are so not up with the times
and I am not proud of it

I avoid a lot of rap music because I am offended by the words they use
as a former combat arms officer and conservative
I am planning to restrict the sale of incandescent light bulbs
and am offended by butt cleavage
and thence by the Turks until 1827

I am offended by things in the paper every day
mundane things like beheadings of Scandinavians
I am personally offended by Smurfs because blue is the color
I am offended by any public display of affection
I am offended by your ability to be offended

let me just finish by saying that yes sometimes I am offended
I am offended by demonic pimps who love how they feel when they save
someone
and I am offended by some of your comments
how dare you claim there is something wrong with Kevin Costner
he's still kind of a man-whore but he's a different man-whore now

It Ain't Easy

Michael Bay is a whorehouse
before the feast of a crashing plane
with some kind of proof that capitalism can blow itself

whoopee! I believe in:
the inherent goodness of all beings
eyes that change color
small tits
open-minded people

I much more hate the idea of consuming power
I'm a "power-consumption-conscious freak"
do you use smiley faces on Mother's Day
well, yesterday was Mother's Day

I never drafted anything but I am capable of handling
extremely emotional situations where I get paid very well
to read the personals and drink Slushees

I'll help anyone who pays me to hint at emotional depth or something
on the other hand I am here for emotional guidance from the dead
few people realize it's difficult to heal
from the emotional distress I experienced this week
by an Indian woman who was complaining about karaoke

I already said it ain't easy and it takes a toll

Enya is a whore

Funnel Whore

what is up funnel whore now what is up
drink enough with a woman and the thing will get
so that spaghetti sauce sprayed out the small end
more and more and MORE!

funnel cake! GARRR give me some now!
I'm guessing whoever it is they made it from scratch
mainly because you can't lay claim to any of it
because that's good too blah

so we wound up at the ultrabicentennial exit forever by a guy
with the worst tan I have ever seen
I burned myself 80 times
and now my cat has
a tube sticking out of his head

why don't you pour rat poison into your mouth?
ma'am, no ma'am

this huge fuck-off big black spider crawls out
from underneath a state punishment apparatus
it looks like the motherfucking apocalypse
I was sure I was going to die with mayonnaise all over myself
what is it with me and spiders?

so image my dismay when I slapped this ferile bitch on
and when she was just lower left until my sustain neighbors on
moving onto ended up facing her for a few showed glide hours
somewhere floating free Rhode Island y'know
and lo and behold
I got chased by Bugs Bunny and he took my soda

I'm Tired of Eating Lunch with Chicks Everyday (Signature, Event, Roast Beef)

hey, bitch, give me some roast beef
screw you, sexist

bitches who can't read for context are of no concern to me
you can't define men without making them separate from structuralist
"hairy chasms"

which is really another way of making the claim that a signifier is haunted
by sustainable earth-friendly Tofurky

for me the way to avoid the abyss
is to pursue a rhetorical low-fat food source

or go to Alaska
writing itself struggles over and over to go here

academic methodologism and paradigm-enforcement is just
far healthier for you than, say, Fresca

Dracula must be a werewolf though Canada for example
never learned how to get down on her knees eating Americans

the generation above getting in morphine and using guns and all that
the way history is conventionally about book proposals

they meet some son of a bitch who studied knife-fighting
they send his soul to psychoanalysis

I'm running with the "theory bitch" moniker
(is Madonna old enough to have a festschrift?)

whatever
what's completely missing is a circular puzzle with no end

and really just leaving out
the beef and seeing how it comes out

Rudolph Fucks the Baloney Off My Nose

—for Maurice Burford

so you want a day off
let's look at what you are asking

Exxon and Sony for hamburger meat but now
we're better off or "fuck Christ" and more to that effect

it's not Rudolph the Red-Nosed Reindeer's fault that
there are no telephones on death row

it seems like only yesterday that Satan welded my crotch shut
patchouli, should we ban that shit, too?

Silliman's Blog is pressed against a smelly load
of guys in LA who have hundreds of millions of dollars

Dennis Cooper starts screaming
& returns to having conventional suck-&-fuck twink-on-twink sex

all we want is a sandwich, some cookies, and an orange
he fuck his boss wife in her tide pussy, Google, page 1

I don't fuck around at those crematoriums
with recent animated movies like *Antz* and *A Bug's Life*

I wouldn't wipe my nose with a swan
I'd rather fuck a chicken

I dress like a princess and always make sure
I owe the government money and have to mail a check

I just asked what the plastic over my nose was for
(I vomited a microwave kebab out of my nose 2 days ago)

an ex-brother-in-law of mine used to tell the funniest joke
about Billie Jean King

date of birth: November 22, 1943
"fucking you so that you'll stay fucked"

Picasso

I am not a whore but many of my friends are
it is an ugly time but they should look at me and vomit
and then probably commit suicide

at age 45 a woman in her early thirties
was very important to my stupid twig bones
under the gaze of that elusive hard-on Picasso

each time you fly you kill a bird
and also you fail for being a little bandwagon
and hating RuneScape

if only I wasn't such a dowager
done up in murders
just like the Babylonian

and as for this white power nonsense
I spent about a year on that game
baby got big and she's gonna get bigger

"but whore's the lodge?" demanded Miss Maria
"hero ma'am" replied Dorcas
these tastes pop and vanish in my mouth

everything on this planet
every toothless polar bear
the name of the blog hasn't changed

reload this page look at me
I am a stupid man
I have nothing

no one cares about my work
I have wasted my life
I guess you could combine spam and football

Why I Am Not a Forest Ranger

I am an exception to the rule, not a forest ranger. I have a belief that my father served in a forest ranger school in Florida and was always "all over blue mold." Scientists are curious, but I am not showing curiosity. Now you can clearly see why I am not employed. I call the said garden mine because I own it (for only I suppose this is why I am loath to talk about how much my moods consume me). I'm not going off the pill. Basically, I didn't realize how stupid it was saying "Ma'am, I am a forest ranger and I am lost." This is why I am not terribly in favor of lithography. I wonder why I am here in China right now at this moment. A nice, vivid reminder to myself of why I am spending all my free time dressed as a birdwatcher: I love watching birds.

The first fact to face is that Unix was developed with a group of people in which some included "Forest Ranger" and "Timelord." Not only is the communication efficient, it is virtually error-free. Sometimes the lab equipment does not need to be purchased. The police officer did not want to report that I am retired forest ranger in 1945. I had to retire prematurely as I was leary of telling many of your gay sisters and brothers that the real grace of the cross comes through a native species that did not become nonnative. They were not bad-ass assassins like people think but rather forest rangers. There is not an historical location referring to the culture. I'm semi-depressed but am trying to keep my chin up. That's why I am asking. I was just saying that this explains why I am getting so many contacts from America coming for example in the sentence: "Lamont never would of bit a forest ranger."

To a millionaire: "You know why I am a good actor, mister? Because I am a failure in the forest." Not so much as a parking ticket shows up until December. This also encourages lateral growth that increases lashes. I batted my eyes at the forest ranger and explained that I was a good kisser. I can only imagine that it was not luxurious enough. I believed with all my heart that I could be a forest ranger, an astronaut. This is why I am disgusted by the BSA's policy towards homosexuals. I might not like the idea of two women but by God I am not going Colorado arsonist all my life. This is why I am not a slave to society as most of you are.

This man sees the immediate trees, sees the fire. I will be understanding why I am learning what I am learning. It will be interesting to me. Forest ranger living on the side of a mountain, you might find out why I am the way I am! Know that the sole reason why I am here today is to provide Joe with a paycheck, to take botany. "I am interested in purchasing all items related to Wyoming at one time. Can you help me? Sincerely, Mary 'Forest Ranger' Shortly." I think you will understand why I am been trying forest ranger hat. Get not riding my bike, but posting. I guess that is why it seems that some people in Uganda are not too happy at the sight and not just as a forest ranger in a forest ranger pickup truck going with this hard time. This exact situation is why I am so disappointed. All this is very interesting to me as I need to advance. I am choosing blindness. This is not going to be easy.

Der Explosion

nothing but downbeat groovery in NASA spacegear
that's what's been holding me together

& women holding doctorates in a series of narrow tunnels
tunnels I could not fit down that's right

then you honed it down with the Abu Ghraib people
& a badly drawn blue goblin holding two axes

wearing clothes & "honkin' down the highway"
(that struck me as not very punk rock)

he is currently holding auditions for teenage girls
funny but you have to see the video he's holding up

what many consider the ultimate wife of David Bowie
these days she's all *Watership Down*

I was seriously thinking of holding a funeral for dinosaurs
who had been heroes of socialist drag queens

I thought there could be no greater guy who was asking me
(unpatriotic Sikh middle name) "ouch"

don't bring me der explosion
I talk not up to par with James Taylor all the way

I like and listen to the prog-rock band Marillion
I am going to lay down for half an hour

The Bowl of Lucky Charms Project

guess what court supervision bitch
all of a sudden like whoa
I got the typical flat maize pancake "tortilla"
spilling from under the rabbit costume
     "aw yeah that does stink"

I had a dream about a kitten last night
I kept trying to put it in the litterbox
and it kept getting away from me somehow
as I put it in the fridge I pulled out a video cassette
"Making Love out of Nothing at All"
(Air Supply) put it in my mouth
     put it in the oven
     in our phony make-believe oven
     an' bake bine a gawnish bastie
     an' he's got one o' the warm tins
     o' beer an' he's put it in the hole
     like Greenspan gave the order
     to crank out 190 billion dollars put it in the banks
     make sure they capitalize it put it in bold print
          repeated for like ever

     I said it would rock if someone
made a clockwork mouse and put it
in the woods to teach me a lesson

Cavemen

cavemen do not like caviar
or black pants and brown socks
the sincerity and sheer downhomeness of their songs
reflects on combat experience and warm tortillas
my favorite is when we cook up their intestines
and use them for chitlins

I can't shake the feeling that I'm watching a little girl
a girl who probably ate chitlins without blinking
but always comes through
with a narcissistic display of "caring"
it's refreshing in this day and age to hear an artist
whose sincerity doesn't grab you

Israeli troops feel obliged
to bash Transcendental Meditation
suicide bombers provide needed irony
can we table that for study?
this is a gardening question, asked
with the utmost sincerity

the places we are from often become places we love
I will put on a straitjacket and eat some chitlins and arugula
and we can discuss your little problems

Modern Love

it's hard to believe but it's
that time of year again when
John F. Kennedy and Laci Peterson buy me a new pancreas

I love a small kitchen because
my name is Frank
and I love a great many things

I fell in love immediately somehow in 2006
watching those pert jiggly things on TV
while they suck the oxygen out of the news cycle

there's nothing better than knowing
that Iran is big and strong
and full of lovin' moms

JonBenet honey you're better off in heaven
nobody loves you like your mama loves you
but who's lovin' your mama

you rock so hard I can barely stand it
have I told you at any point lately
that I absolutely love your photography

Hard Lovin' Anne Frank

damn I wish the *Garden State* soundtrack didn't kick so much ass
stop telling me Anne Frank is some kind
          of bomb-ass pussy
single mother chat rooms make my skin creep
New Orleans looks like a burnt snowman
most importantly later in life be yourself

downtown there are folks
filling out educational forms
who will pay you to put your panties on their faces

meanwhile over in West Des Moines
I distinctly recall three *Star Trek* novels dealing specifically
with a giant polar bear who smoked too much weed
snooping into the contents of a 9" x 7" x 5"
full-color embossed metal Conan lunchbox

Mr Hollywood has always been in the habit
of banging retarded beyotches
with invisible thermal underwear
he is a hot Nazi (a hotzi if you will)

nothing says lovin' like a large blow-up photo of Anne Frank
not Black History Month beach vacations
not Hannah Arendt lampshades
not one of the 10 million reasons
I'm afraid to ask

Heavy Horses

I live out in the country with my wife Theresa
in a little factory that makes baby dolls
for marginal people living under motorways during the war
people who like horse voodoo
I can't help feeling they're desperate retards
a bunch of solid wood optical mouse pads

Matthew Broderick breaks his collarbone falling off
this German No-Wave project with no foundation
firing guns at criminals making them sick
this oblique reference to screwing is an attempt
to protest about the type of horse he used to fix the lightbulb
regarding the lyrical content his stuff is stinky brown
these "human horses" prefer the intestine

a single human skeleton gets inserted
in all sorts of places
riding at horse-and-buggy pace
into a vast web of history
these few seconds repeated indefinitely
in a list of terrariums essentially
that lend bounce to horses and (on the other hand) kangaroos

broken-down horses have sucked me through a vortex
and into the basement
next to me I have my own magical pile of little colored girl

time to make some glue
we need to make glue from this horse

Dear Police Officer

you don't know who I am but
I am a straight-up person and I am going tell you thing
"I am a mom" and I work from home
I sent out an email asking some questions
to formulate a scenario as to what
may be written with burnt remains
on the backs of some chairs
in a way-possible laid-back mode
now that jubilation is replaced

I want to stop by and say stuff to you
I want not to tell but I must
I don't wanna not tell you thing
maybe we heard nothing
maybe something
but I can tell you thing much—

if you really want to know
this book is horrible they tell you thing
no-charge, thing you should know long time
but I think you not know
even how they made butter

I feel my angry feelings
I guess I do not like Jeff or what he represents

don't be a fool and listen to the people

have you lost any of your cattle right
in front of the Seattle Federal Sending Station
                or what

Men

I'm working like a beaver
I worked all my life
and still have to work

before, what looked like a deer
had a bill like a duck
it was like Eavan Boland or something

all men are liars
traitors and whores
they laugh all the way to the bank

earthquakes are good
there are free unicorn rides
less and less everyday

Write Like a Beaver

you're not twenty-one any longer, and at your age—
a little man like a beaver—
how wonderful to write like that!

your encouragement of English literature
enables me to get somewhat cheesed
at what these people write
like, *Lord of the Rings*

three men and a maid
knew what he was talking about
so that's why I'm wondering

him gnawed at his own fingernails
and some crunchy French bread and
we stared at it for a good 5 minutes

I think when I write like a weirdo it comes out better
please try to write like I do

Gene Kelly

hey look at me, I'm Gene Kelly
I'm freaking the pork formica
I'm going to beat the hell out of some pork chops

I've been to Kansas, the creationist state
there were all sorts of Jell-O books in there
featuring such hot stuff as meat

the beehived Pleistocene waitress
served white wine out of her palms
they were visibly shaking, she was freaking out

just some moderately hot woman rock climbing
her naked ass sitting on the impulse doughnuts
in this world that looks better as a blonde

something that isn't beef or chicken had slammed Todd's head
a leaf ($7)
he whined like a girl

this isn't your typical rabbit offal on toast
it's like throwing a pork chop into a kennel
it is that good

Untitled

"exactly who are you and why is it
you have brought this wood here?"
Ray gestured at the pile of wood

he's a maniac, maaaniac on the floor sexual
he would live fast and hard and burn
himself up then folks would say goddam
like you can discourage him
just by punching him in the face

broken hymen of a priest in disguise
with a pregnant girlfriend
Buddy had taken pictures of
them pulling down their jeans

she was a white woman of some "smoky days"
"soiled hands" and
"vacant"
"smell of steaks"
Calgary where dinosaurs left mystery

"persists to throb in my head"
is iambic tetrameter
not pentameter

is everything fricking untitled

oh yeah right who's going
to worship a rock she replied
I love this job

No, *My* Name Is Gary Sullivan, *I* Own a Mansion and a Yacht

hello, violently happy pantyhose tutor!
(she is this little Björk-like elfy fairy girl
and he is a little kid with a tail)

I think Björk is pretty hot

I switched bikes and pedalled over to
the progressive buccaneer coupon fitness battle
I must do things ASAP
(most people have heard of ASAP)
when I got home all we had was meteorology

hallucinating housewives retail alphabet water
interpreting Rush lyrics while peeing
they take the bus
they suddenly realize that peeing on the baked duck
before eating four pieces of toast
is one of the most beautiful love stories

Happiness Is

sharing a book of poetry
a shade tree
a bowl of cherries
it's easy to drown my mother, she has syphilis

I don't expect every day to be great
I don't think anything of a wolverine
sprung from prison on a legal technicality
                creative license
you can find that between *boathouse rental*
and *celebrity deathmatch* in the dictionary

a favorite thing to do for the armed gangs around here
is colorful soaring hard-rock soundscapes
I tote in my guitar and teach them that "doe a deer" song
that'll cook their bowl of cherries

full sweet sensual
               juicy
          cherries *mmm*!
[see fruit plate below]

the Kiss Army's no good at counting money anymore
the eyes of a deer see best on the head of an ape
proving once again that *Cahiers du Cinema* is for assholes

currently we are having an epidemic
of fake-titted neglected liberal thinkers
life not bowl of cherries for man hit by car!
unless there is a pirate ship without Kevin Spacey
   "har, me hearties"

understanding how a rainbow works, yo
God is making fun of you

also it being Bastille Day I made a pilgrimage
also because for dinner last night I had a bowl of cherries
a bowl of cherries, that's healthy

Poems About Trees

I have written a couple of poems about trees
poems about trees and snakes and lakes and birds
poems about nature and life in New England
I write crappy poems and eat babies
if you like poems about trees you're in for a treat

when I get nervous I get hyper and bump into people
I read to them what MapQuest gave me
round during then in the mom seeker panties
to help me narrow down the slut thing word jobs
rawr I'm too stupid to be able to make my point clear

if you for critique you eventually works at what a
chromosome disorder speech theory itch be responsible
congratulations, really nice birth control
is the most important challenge to vintage porn food stamps
and then I thought only God etc. (i.e. chemicals about progesterone)

the woods are full of police
90% Khalil Gibran, 10% carved wooden men
that can see souls at night
but I, warlike, considering gray cream for attire
enjoying impossible "nudes on ice," more death

as though your hands were hollow and sequently
the big soprano going back to her church
because her crazy French mom does and no one knows why
brainwashed creationists go ever yodeling to attract
the jolly echo of a forest of orange sauce
"you anus look like a chicken pie"
I hate you, dig me up

people write poems about trees and the words
are shaped like a tree

kids are stupid
$10

A Walrus Doing a Duck

I never write anything anymore and when I did
it blew ass worse than a walrus doing a duck
Ian and Liz think they're the best
looking thoughtful begins unpicking her
under the blazing sun so high

John Cusack gets mistaken for a bear ... Humphrey the Bear
my friend saw your profile and thinks you force him
under the flailing hooves and shining blade
doing sudoku
you can get the equivalent of mock-duck sans the can

walrus on my plane? explode
I'm watchin' it
literally, it was a feast
down below my mother cries
mean duck loves an ocean

wowies! or ambulances
I'm taking my anger at RealPlayer out on you
what I'm doing is playing Sir Walter Ralegh
I know we all have to go to college
which totally I have to learn so many things

Zed's hasty shots cause the men to buy the group
that guy needs to see the video of the walrus
come on guy!
what's is that walrus doing?
I am bored

I'm not making a scene
I am trying to respect The Beatles
these kids are like, Mommy Mommy
what's is The Beatles doing?
please, please what? please what?

Yankee Doodle Fuck Machine

I am a robot and I'm angry at people
I'm not wasting a vacation on a Boy Scout jamboree
the songs I can play are "Für Elise,"
"The Entertainer," and "Fuck You Becky"

Anne Murray is the ugliest boy
I have ever seen in my life
"he is optimistic that man will come out on top"
where the fuck is my time machine

regardless of how "indisputable" it may seem
to the "fags" or "Arabs" or whatever
we all have to have "banks" and as such banks get
to fuck up politics in America and the "world"

"at night we ride through mansions of glory
in suicide machines ... and fuck them," Flaubert wrote
in his journal with a little *riiipp*! *AUGH*! *whap whap*
whap whap whap as he sat in his gold Rolls-Royce

poems from Kansas don't have to be that crazy
one of them is "Yankee Doodle," the other one isn't
then cowboy change your ways today or with us you will ride
keep your stick on the ice, go fuck yourself

there are over 100 words for "shit"
and only one for "fuck you"
and every one of the self-serve machines at Kinko's
is an Anne Of Green Gables pop-up dollhouse

"I was forced to eat your average American"

I was forced to eat your average American
in my case when I chew I find it
to be a challenge I lube my meats
to name one benefit it's hot

have you not had oiled socks?
come throw me in the air
for teenage cingular customers
for dogs receive welfare

but the little devil did not seem to barf
such pristine sort of fare at all
but here is an toenail he desires
to snore you the dreamiest

and we decided the best place
for him to barf was in the little jeep

Like Decorations in a Wigger Cemetery

a man named Wigger was reported today
to have gone to his death

he began to crawl in a curious way
using his powerful shoulders and arms

shoes made of flesh was sacked and remained
in ruined polygonal wabs in a fair state

on which is the royal unicorn rampant
one of few or only fixtures in a lamp

that holds three bulbs or more stupid animals pictures
stupid-animals-pictures

white plastic, how wonderful it made you engulf it
after frequenting any space decorated in a Feng Shui manner

after frequenting any space decorated
in a Feng Shui manner, you will feel … blueberry

overnight-in-a-haunted-house
turkey vultures fly into the area

three-piece cushions that costs $20 elsewhere
priest with a boner from *Little Mermaid*

how to Space Ghost video in Space Ghost video
The Best of Silverchair, Vol. 1

hung-up Daisy-Duck
lean-on-me-original-singer ventilated hardhats

the Rosedale Cemetery ass from
the Rosedale Cemetery ass

old guys ruin authentic Polish recipes
that was what Lalo had heard

Necronomicon

"Necronomicon"
that's what my 11-foot-tall unicorn's name would be

my unicorn tells me every day that all white people are racist
I have to go slide down the rainbow in my backyard
so hot Asian guys can put a Megadeth decal on my favorite ice cream

people interested in theology have to put a goatee on my unicorn
in order for it to stand correctly
I'm going to temporarily get some new rocks as a present

I wish my dad would be cool when my unicorn comes over tonight

I ran down the hill because I was worried about my unicorn
but I also confess that I wanted to get some herbal medicine
I took a vow that bards with harps and flutes
would never melt my journey when undefined

my lover girl and I made friends partly with our resident linguist
George Lakoff is a professor at UC Berkeley
and relies on a cathedral to find his hotel
"a slight pause occurs when two immediately adjacent vowels
in consecutive syllables are pronounced"
by using a prefix and being really philosophical I can live in Russia

the people who loved my slide show
are actually controlled by unicorns

an old woman being led through the parking lot by two girls
speaks in energetic explanatory bursts
she is oppressing my unicorn
she colonized my unicorn
and she's gone now

Blank Verse

oh you must think blank verse
is the place you see in your head
when thirteen boy scouts use that antenna
to give a muscly lad the what-for
right up the old cantonal rhinotracheitis
somewhere in heaven

in the end the average Joe takes it in the poop chute
laughing on cat grass
and the sexy police woman costume
may be incompatible with our language

Foucault's three-volume history of birthday cake design
sends me thinking of other things
never commit to an ideology
pick a more obscure philosopher
always carry pocket knives
to clear brush I won't shoot lawyers but
you have to take them to New Jersey

western society is what scabies looks like
bad, normative
it's so sick it's a subacid crab nebula

contemplative how it got there?
whatever, hooker, you're used to it

I'm going to be so damn ready America
but I really have to get to the hospital

Total Elephant Molestation

—for Gary Sullivan

an election like this is like eating an elephant
the two gentlemen cause the total to come out complicated
not that I'm advocating "total elephant molestation"
well, okay, maybe I am

the general public is being molested in a Burger King bathroom
if Miami found a cure for pedophilia
many offspring of perverts will do the reverse
pay the molester $200 and sit in free parking
where it's brave showing weaknesses in public

for the better good of society we need to tell the ACLU
to lay off the symbol of a little girl growing up
Satanic homosexuals in the Boy Scouts
stand as a beacon of enlightened molestation

you don't understand about pro-choice women
what was I to suppose when I found myself
growing a tank
but I would not have come now to molest you, Flora
and now I think of it, the sooner I get to W_____ the better

a total stranger gets on a motorcycle
in the middle of winter and drives 300 miles
child molesters rape children
big fucking difference

The Mohawk Lumber Company

my dad had a subroutine for his tank's behavior, I had a subroutine for mine
it looks like I will get a better deal from one company if I have my own tank
the Mohawk Lumber Company is building and erecting a new tank
a burrowing tank they can ride down into the earth's crust

I can't afford this lack of interest to hatch into my barn
perhaps you could put on a wife-beater instead
of sitting by an earthen tank huffing airplane glue
in a sandwich bag and waiting for birds

there are three things which do not concern the reader:
snakes, internal body parts, and
the song I actually have heard
on my local rock station only once in a great while

Spider-Man acid just happened to be the kind of acid
that only came to my region every once in a great while
back when the tops of my boobs peeked out of my tank top
the only way to free China is by lovingly stroking stray cats

we all know talking to people is fraught with peril
it's worse than dogs making love
you're always welcome to visit my skull
in your pink terrycloth shorts that only reinforce
your position as an authority making demands

all motion is relative
big deal, you know what makes me happy?
when a child is placed into a small box

I will make you eat a bath towel

Complications

Napoleon was not afraid of lions
when he saw it was only a lion he cried out
with the soft mouth of someone young nineteen maybe

"I'm not afraid of lions
I'm not afraid of anything
really I'm not afraid of lions"

Tarzan naturally is not afraid of lions
but his leading ladies often are
when their routine is interrupted

Tarzan was sitting with the window open
leaning out the window for another photo
"no, that is not a good picture of me"

a patient who was not afraid of lions told Freud
"I am not afraid of lions because they attack directly
I am afraid of insects because they attack indirectly"

he challenged us to be in closer contact
with all lions so that all lions see
what it can do for the whole thing

_____ was not afraid of lions but he was afraid of sin
he was not afraid of vanity but he had some doubt
he could have fought with a lion

he could fight with the lion barehanded
he had a nervous breakdown
life is very complicated

As I Walked Out

I see by your outfit that you are a cowboy.
I'm not a cowboy, but I am a lesbian.
Everyone calls me "Smitty"

I see by your Minnesota test that you are inclined
towards a cowboy suit with matched pistols and a pink leotard,
one Happy Meal, three bank robbers, and two pirates from various
Fisher-Price sets.

I see by your smiley face that you are a person of rare intellect and wit—
a man of thoughtfulness, a man who cares,
a cowboy with his hands high in the air!

I see by your chart that you've been recommended for dismissal.
You were thrown out of this city because you were a cowboy and almost
was shot.
It's very clear by your comments here that you are not a cop.

I see by your avatar that you are a Troy Aikman fan.
We set forth to confront the nation and lend a cowboy's hand
but I would also be very upset if one of them was shot by a cop by mistake.

I see by your list you are a "coneflower" fan.
I love them as well and should be grateful I'm allowed to walk the earth…
of course nobody knows when I'm going to stop living.

I see by your accent that you are Norvegian.
I believe your story. One time I saw a ghost of a cowboy.
I did a broadcast about this.

I see by your knowledge of the Tiger Cub Motto
that you want big bucks for having a cowboy day camp.
You're a cowboy-hat-wearing fool!

I see by your license you are from Oklahoma.
The worst piece of ass I ever had came from Oklahoma.
She is downstairs, watching a cowboy cooking show, laughing.

I see by your blank stare that you watch a lot of TV,
two neanderthals using the term "old metal."

(it was a cowboy film).

I see by your expression I've hit it at last.
By your standards I must be a water buffalo.
When I was a kid I wanted to be an old negro with his hands on his hips.

I see by your expression you disapprove and are ready to quarrel with me,
and sure, maybe there's something you'll learn or you'll see.
Saul was a cowboy before he was a king.

Unspace

this ineffable vehicle slurping its way through unspace
not only has a salad bar, it has a whole Sears from 1898

(I just hit several people
who aren't Jason Priestley)

can you imagine sitting in the back of the vehicle and
your kidnappers have amazing flying skills

in an alternate world where Hitler
was fascinated by anything to do with online divorce

wonder also why media won't highlight the huge CGI locust
he was wanting to look at a vehicle and said he was from a town

he look at his hands and said something
"uh huh what up old man"

then all the futuristic squid people will be all like
"uh huh we've got the best health care plan there is"

you know those rubber prosthesis things they sell in sex stores
that are like pieces of white brontosaurus

and just out of curiosity
how much do those things cost

it's so mushy, it's so mushy, it's so mushy
some of this sounds a bit like that

we think it's in the best interests of the country
that more people explode

any vehicle that doesn't get it
we're going to tax that vehicle

Against Sasquatch

If anyone had a grudge against Sasquatch
it would be the folks running this somewhat remote lodge

some inanimate objects have nothing
but you can't get that anymore

or better yet why not shed
a layer of skin, jump into battle

same way with Thor, doesn't matter
if he has the hammer or not

to deliver what the narrator
calls the "death blow"

the main knock is he's got
the activation click to find

secret wars? or some other
final piece of the globe of life

a corollary of this is chimps'
and gorillas' lack of swimming ability

but I doubt he freely mentions monkeys
but back in the past

I was so close to dying
a person has to continue

both her and
her home transforming to dust

I honestly try to describe the item
and I will now state simply

that I have nothing against Sasquatch
he's always been cool to me

Organic/Ultra-Organic

travelling through the late 1970's and early 1980's
as the Saxon made his way through apartments
the proteges had the power of the air long ago
before the oldest was young and big and little

the bordering palaces were obliged to fall
with predatory can-do tracheotomy that I didn't do with a Bic pen
even more skull-like than the anti-NY *Planet of the Apes* bias
(or Jean-Luc Godard?) anyway, this is not very scientific

I am off topic I'm entirely biased but I think
young companies tap into the power of Brad Pitt watching the sun rise
partly because of how radical he is and how subversive he is
we think of him as kind of stinky

apparently I woke up one morning
in uber-super-mega-ultra-fucktard mode
some douchebag bitches had a party at 97 Something Street
I saw a woman breastfeeding a puppy

I took geography for a reason
I do like the globe my god I like the globe
I sometimes sit around boundless as the sea
I haven't seen *Cabin Fever* sounds good though

being a witch I hate the beach
the ocean is a buried zero
so now I try and not fuck anyone over or take advantage
cuz sometimes I do dumb shit that I hate

fat American you suck
and your stepdad is such an asshole
a naive tw@t has her head shoved so far up her own a$$
I'm surprised she can see the really scary stuff

what do you like?
"I like animals"
would you be willing to read a book about animals?
I try hard but I can't understand it

the trouble is I don't speak or read Olde English
nor was I actually taught Olde English
anyway I rather poke holes into myself
with a rusty fork than read anything

who would believe that Scarlett Johansson's breasts were not a dog
her breasts that were like electric cougars
she reluctantly will show her breasts in the movie
while trying to freeze bats into hibernation

the cute puppy you once knew has become
an ex-gym teacher with a master's degree in education
everyone calls me Andy
today is my birthday, pa rum pa pum pum

on the web is the uber-snarky
"people's distributed guano-thrower"
of course the argyle pattern for my account of the manure
that is to say miniature espresso machines

because I *like* my landlord
he's bright and happy and listens to *Dark Side of the Moon* a lot
you know why? the mind numbing dullness
and repetitive nature along with "fabulous filim!"

isn't it rich aren't we a pair
Sondheim ululated weaponless Cheyennes
Liverpool underpants thumping guacamole Arab breastplate
jackass library beer information Guantanamo sibling meh

you are a nun! and it really blows
duh duh duh I am Brady hate me forever
yellow baby table Girl Scout badgers bad bitch Boy Scout zippers
I don't even know what I am thinking anymore

this is not the military
I don't have time to look up something
most e-mailed useless echinacea is the union but
global warming is happening

I make out with my pillow that's probably what happens
I eat rice a lot and I used to eat ice cubes for dessert
I am searching for romance and desire
I'd say that most people don't know that about me

A Cloud in Haggar Slacks

man climbs hill and dives into ocean
his blue fellingus commands attention
the cloud descends like a rock
into Haggar slacks Grandma smuggles
and she loved to sing hymns

and predict the internet will not
translate to fibro fogs of Piaget quotes
so every cloud of beef
could make sure you're not
walking out with an armful of hanging executions

the the gas and dust around
misses' hidden iced-tea
videocassette recorder leave me recently
I should say & the state I think
they will be pretty I will guarantee

so some pallbearers will be retired
elk-laminated roofing shingles
control hair cancer more than you want
to know however meow anemia
the "slimming solution"

types of insects ruining the Canada/Israel
experience of early human development
zip carefully from the fact
that I am gone to go and look at a company
I hope I am never reborn and iridescent

Sioux Formlessness

I guess I feel like articulating
the poetics behind dead people
which live on our eyelashes

about noon I preached at New-Mills to an earnest artless loving people
and in the evening at poor dull dead Stockport
not without hopes

there was this thick
emptiness
a real dead air there

unornamented moorlands
confirmed exotic violences
rowboat traders

Sioux formlessness
Olivia de Havilland Olivia Newton John
Mary Reilly Mary Reilly

imagine what could happen
if the dissolved remains of an evil cyclops
is looking for his next meal

falling back into the pointlessly nostalgic cyborg prostitute
sex pregnancy China economy laughin' cryin' massage music
Christian school kissin' cousins

every one was an 'Enery
so strangely repellent
so poetic and so videoplus

then Byron died
and Tennyson scratched on a rock
"Byron is dead"

Dusty the Oncologist

thanks for sending me your poems
I enjoyed reading your obscurely-worded
classical pieces of paper issued by black women
dating back to the late 1800s

this is a long one
well I did make a commitment to this so here goes
as my eyes were closing here were these amazing lines
"a frozen path / a path concealed in autumn"

may you write many more beautiful poems and songs
from Colorado's Rockies
the cancer appears to be gone
I'll be referring you to the chief of oncology

I don't know how many oranges spill out into the street
following the dopey adventures of a small brown thing
that tumbled from an industry where "reality" is a movie
that turned me off to dental work forever

I wonder what people don't know about
getting men to wash their hands in public restrooms
in hopes that they want to be great at something
oh no not us we go up every road and have a cuppa

why in blazes would a man walk down a hot road
with his private parts hanging out
when he saw something on a pile of wood or something
it was basically high noon and I was jogging

another interesting part of this is that at no time
are the streets outside filled with rickshaws and patriarchy
people like me don't even have the chance
to resurrect their parents

I have another successful faucet attached to canvas tarps
mostly a pink variety with a dark liter of IV fluid
and a very nice official cremation certificate
I wish those old boxes would stay stuck in their corners

the poem is in its way a confession and
all the heavyweight policy wonks can't believe it
I'm now the richest man in town
because of the military insurance

"death is not a diagnosis"
just an inherent momentum rolling down empty highways
it's a God thing
except there's not that extra step

I've learned the hard way that some poems don't rhyme
I was thinking I'd like that poem about cat feet sung at my funeral
since Dusty isn't here I have to add
it was like heaven to have those shade trees

ROOF BOOKS

the best in language since 1976

Titles

- Andrews, Bruce. **Co**. Collaborations with Barbara Cole, Jesse Freeman, Jessica Grim, Yedda Morrison, Kim Rosefield. 104p. $12.95.
- Andrews, Bruce. **Ex Why Zee**. 112p. $10.95.
- Andrews, Bruce. **Getting Ready To Have Been Frightened**. 116p. $7.50.
- Arakawa, Gins, Madeline. **Making Dying Illegal**. 224p. $22.95.
- Benson, Steve. **Blue Book**. Copub. with The Figures. 250p. $12.50
- Bernstein, Charles. **Controlling Interests**. 80p. $11.95.
- Bernstein, Charles. **Islets/Irritations**. 112p. $9.95.
- Bernstein, Charles (editor). **The Politics of Poetic Form**. 246p. $12.95; cloth $21.95.
- Brossard, Nicole. **Picture Theory**. 188p. $11.95.
- Cadiot, Olivier. **Former, Future, Fugitive**. Translated by Cole Swensen. 166p. $13.95.
- Champion, Miles. **Three Bell Zero**. 72p. $10.95.
- Child, Abigail. **Scatter Matrix**. 79p. $9.95.
- Davies, Alan. **Active 24 Hours**. 100p. $5.
- Davies, Alan. **Signage**. 184p. $11.
- Davies, Alan. **Rave**. 64p. $7.95.
- Day, Jean. **A Young Recruit**. 58p. $6.
- Di Palma, Ray. **Motion of the Cypher**. 112p. $10.95.
- Di Palma, Ray. **Raik**. 100p. $9.95.
- Doris, Stacy. **Kildare**. 104p. $9.95.
- Doris, Stacy. **Cheerleader's Guide to the World: Council Book** 88p. $12.95.
- Dreyer, Lynne. **The White Museum**. 80p. $6.
- Dworkin, Craig. **Strand**. 112p. $12.95.
- Dworkin, Craig, editor. **The Consequence of Innovation: 21st Century Poetics**. 304p. $29.95.
- Edwards, Ken. **Good Science**. 80p. $9.95.
- Eigner, Larry. **Areas Lights Heights**. 182p. $12, $22 (cloth).
- Fitterman, Robert. **Rob the Plagiarist**. 108p. $13.95
- Gardner, Drew. **Petroleum Hat**. 96p. $12.95.
- Gizzi, Michael. **Continental Harmonies**. 96p. $8.95.
- Gladman, Renee. **A Picture-Feeling**. 72p. $10.95.
- Goldman, Judith. **Vocoder**. 96p. $11.95.
- Gordon, Nada. **Folly**. 128p. $13.95
- Gottlieb, Michael. **Ninety-Six Tears**. 88p. $5.
- Gottlieb, Michael. **Gorgeous Plunge**. 96p. $11.95.
- Gottlieb, Michael. **Lost & Found**. 80p. $11.95.
- Greenwald, Ted. **Jumping the Line**. 120p. $12.95.
- Grenier, Robert. **A Day at the Beach**. 80p. $6.

- Grosman, Ernesto. **The XULReader: An Anthology of Argentine Poetry (1981–1996)**. 167p. $14.95.
- Guest, Barbara. **Dürer in the Window, Reflexions on Art.** Book design by Richard Tuttle. Four color throughout. 80p. $24.95.
- Hills, Henry. **Making Money**. 72p. $7.50. VHS videotape $24.95. Book & tape $29.95.
- Huang Yunte. **SHI: A Radical Reading of Chinese Poetry**. 76p. $9.95
- Hunt, Erica. **Local History**. 80 p. $9.95.
- Kuszai, Joel (editor) **poetics@**, 192 p. $13.95.
- Inman, P. **Criss Cross**. 64 p. $7.95.
- Inman, P. **Red Shift**. 64p. $6.
- Lazer, Hank. **Doublespace**. 192 p. $12.
- Levy, Andrew. **Paper Head Last Lyrics**. 112 p. $11.95.
- Mac Low, Jackson. **Representative Works: 1938–1985**. 360p. $18.95 (cloth).
- Mac Low, Jackson. **Twenties**. 112p. $8.95.
- McMorris, Mark. **The Café at Light**. 112p. $12.95.
- Moriarty, Laura. **Rondeaux**. 107p. $8.
- Nasdor, Marc. **Sonnetailia**. 80p. $12.95
- Neilson, Melanie. **Civil Noir**. 96p. $8.95.
- Osman, Jena. **An Essay in Asterisks**. 112p. $12.95.
- Pearson, Ted. **Planetary Gear**. 72p. $8.95.
- Perelman, Bob. **Virtual Reality**. 80p. $9.95.
- Perelman, Bob. **The Future of Memory**. 120p. $14.95.
- Perelman, Bob. **Iflife**. 140p. $13.95.
- Piombino, Nick, **The Boundary of Blur**. 128p. $13.95.
- Price, Larry. **The Quadragene**. 72p. $12.95.
- Prize Budget for Boys, **The Spectacular Vernacular Revue**. 96p. $14.95.
- Raworth, Tom. **Clean & Will-Lit**. 106p. $10.95.
- Reilly, Evelyn. **Styrofoam**. 72p. $12.95.
- Robinson, Kit. **Balance Sheet**. 112p. $11.95.
- Robinson, Kit. **Democracy Boulevard**. 104p. $9.95.
- Robinson, Kit. **Ice Cubes**. 96p. $6.
- Rosenfield, Kim. **Good Morning—MIDNIGHT—**. 112p. $10.95.
- Scalapino, Leslie. **Objects in the Terrifying Tense Longing from Taking Place**. 88p. $9.95.
- Seaton, Peter. **The Son Master**. 64p. $5.
- Shaw, Lytle, editor. **Nineteen Lines: A Drawing Center Writing Anthology**. 336p. $24.95
- Sherry, James. **Popular Fiction**. 84p. $6.
- Silliman, Ron. **The New Sentence**. 200p. $10.
- Silliman, Ron. **N/O**. 112p. $10.95.
- Smith, Rod. **Music or Honesty**. 96p. $12.95
- Smith, Rod. **Protective Immediacy**. 96p. $9.95
- Stefans, Brian Kim. **Free Space Comix**. 96p. $9.95
- Stefans, Brian Kim. **Kluge**. 128p. $13.95
- Sullivan, Gary. **PPL in a Depot**. 104p. $13.95
- Tarkos, Christophe. **Ma Langue est Poétique—Selected Works**. 96p. $12.95.
- Templeton, Fiona. **Cells of Release**. 128p. with photographs. $13.95.
- Templeton, Fiona. **YOU—The City**. 150p. $11.95.
- Torre, Mónica de la. **Public Domain** 104 p. $13.95.

- Torres, Edwin. **The All-Union Day of the Shock Worker**. 112 p. $10.95.
- Tysh, Chris. **Cleavage**. 96p. $11.95.
- Ward, Diane. **Human Ceiling**. 80p. $8.95.
- Ward, Diane. **Relation**. 64p. $7.50.
- Watson, Craig. **Free Will**. 80p. $9.95.
- Watten, Barrett. **Progress**. 122p. $7.50.
- Weiner, Hannah. **We Speak Silent**. 76 p. $9.95
- Weiner, Hannah. **Page**. 136 p. $12.95
- Wellman, Mac. **Miniature**. 112 p. $12.95
- Wellman, Mac. **Strange Elegies**. 96 p. $12.95
- Wolsak, Lissa. **Pen Chants**. 80p. $9.95.
- Yasusada, Araki. **Doubled Flowering: From the Notebooks of Araki Yasusada**. 272p. $14.95.

ROOF BOOKS are published by
Segue Foundation
300 Bowery • New York, NY 10012
Visit our website at **seguefoundation.com**

ROOF BOOKS are distributed by
SMALL PRESS DISTRIBUTION
1341 Seventh Street • Berkeley, CA. 94710-1403.
Phone orders: 800-869-7553
spdbooks.org